A World of Opportunity
International Trade Secrets for Wealth-Builders

Table of Contents

1. Introduction 1

2. Global Opportunities: Understanding International Trade 2

   2.1. Understanding the Basic Concepts of International Trade 2

   2.2. The Role of Trade Agreements in Global Trading 3

   2.3. The Importance of Trade Barriers and Tariffs 3

   2.4. International Trade's Effect on the Global Economy 4

   2.5. Role of International Organizations in Global Trade 4

   2.6. Beyond Goods: The Rise of Global Service Trade 5

   2.7. Future Trends Shaping Global Trade 5

3. Decoding Trade Agreements: A Wealth Builder's Guide 6

   3.1. Importance of Trade Agreements 6

   3.2. Anatomy of a Trade Agreement 6

   3.3. Unveiling Tariff Concessions 7

   3.4. Navigating Non-Tariff Barriers 7

   3.5. Leveraging Trade Facilitation Measures 8

   3.6. Dispute Resolution Mechanisms 8

   3.7. Comprehending Trade in Services 8

   3.8. Understanding Intellectual Property Rights 9

   3.9. Assessing Environmental and Labor Provisions 9

4. Currency Trading and International Business: Minimizing Risk and Maximizing Return 10

   4.1. Understanding the Basics of Currency Trading 10

   4.2. Identifying Currency Risk in International Business 11

   4.3. Strategies to Minimize Currency Risk: Foreign Exchange Hedging 11

   4.4. Leveraging Currency Trading for Profit 11

   4.5. Spot and Future Markets in Currency Trading 12

5. Investing in Overseas Markets: A Comprehensive Approach 14

5.1. Understanding the International Investment Landscape 14

5.2. Evaluating Overseas Investment Opportunities 15

5.3. Planning the Investment 16

5.4. Implementing the Investment Strategy 16

5.5. Navigating Challenges 16

6. Breaking Down Language Barriers for Trade Success 18

6.1. Understanding the Importance of Language in
International Trade 18

6.2. Strategies to Overcome Language Barriers 19

6.3. Cultural Sensitivity and Ethical Communication in Business. 20

6.4. Language Planning for Businesses 20

7. Trade Laws: Navigating Through Foreign Legal Waters 22

7.1. Understand The Legal Framework 22

7.2. Research National Laws 22

7.3. Familiarize Yourself With The Trade Agreements 23

7.4. Seek Legal Counsel 23

7.5. Compliance And Ethics 24

8. Spotting Bubbles and Crashes: Safeguarding Investments
Globally 25

8.1. The Anatomy of Economic Bubbles 25

8.2. Recognizing Economic Bubbles 26

8.3. The Anatomy of Market Crashes 26

8.4. Spotting Market Crashes 27

8.5. Safeguarding Your Investments 27

9. Emerging Markets: The Untapped Goldmines 29

9.1. Deciphering the Dynamics of Emerging Markets 29

9.2. Identifying High-Potential Markets 30

9.3. Crafting an Effective Entry Strategy 31

9.4. Navigating Risks and Challenges 31

9.5. Harnessing Local Resources for Global Progress 32

10. Sustainable Trade: Linking Profits and the Planet 33

    10.1. The Concept of Sustainable Trade 33

    10.2. Sustainable Trade: A Business Case 34

    10.3. Interplay between Free Trade and Sustainable Trade 34

    10.4. The Role of Governments and International Institutions . . . 35

    10.5. Examples of Sustainable Trade Practices 36

11. Future Markets: Understanding Tech Innovations in
International Trade 37

    11.1. The Onward March of Technology 37

    11.2. Electronic Trade Documents 37

    11.3. Massive Data and Predictive Analytics 38

    11.4. The Role of IoT in International Trade 38

    11.5. Artificial Intelligence (AI) Revolution 38

    11.6. Augmented and Virtual Reality 39

    11.7. Tech Innovations and Regulatory Environment 39

    11.8. Conclusion: Envisioning the Future 39

Chapter 1. Introduction

Step into an exciting world of global potential with our special report, "A World of Opportunity: International Trade Secrets for Wealth-Builders". This eye-opening edition unlocks the gateway to prosperity, revealing tips, tricks, and indispensable knowledge about international trade. But this is more than just a guide; it's your ticket to understand global markets and learn how they can work to your advantage, all written in an engaging and accessible style. The wealth-building secrets we unveil are both practical and profound, empowering you to create pathways to success. So why wait? Embark on this captivating journey of economic discovery and let's build your wealth across borders, together!

Chapter 2. Global Opportunities: Understanding International Trade

International trade operates within an intricately woven global marketplace, booming with undiscovered potential and diverse, dynamic opportunities. This comprehensive exploration of international trade will help you fully grasp its intricacies and gather the tools to make it work to your advantage.

2.1. Understanding the Basic Concepts of International Trade

It is of fundamental importance to unbox the core concepts behind international trade. It involves the exchange of goods, services, and capital across international borders or territories. The major elements that compose international trade can be broken down into imports (goods bought from foreign markets) and exports (goods sold to foreign markets).

The basic principles of international trade are grounded in two primary economic theories:

1. Comparative Advantage: This theory, derived from the economist David Ricardo's work, explains that countries should specialise in producing goods or services they can produce relatively more efficiently (i.e., at a lower opportunity cost) and trade with other countries that produce other goods more efficiently.

2. Absolute Advantage: Adam Smith's concept states that countries should produce what they can make the most efficiently and

trade for those goods they can't.

Overall, these theories emphasise the potential benefits of trading goods and services in an international framework, creating a network of comparative and absolute advantages that drives global economic efficiency.

2.2. The Role of Trade Agreements in Global Trading

Trade agreements are pivotal in the world of international trade. These are treaties between two or more nations agreeing on terms of trade between them. Trade agreements often aim to reduce or eliminate tariffs, quota restrictions, and other barriers to free trade.

An example is the North American Free Trade Agreement (NAFTA), which was designed to boost trade among the United States, Canada, and Mexico by eliminating most tariffs on products traded between them. Numerous other trade agreements, such as the European Union and the African Continental Free Trade Agreement (AfCFTA), also exist leading to shaping global trade dynamics.

2.3. The Importance of Trade Barriers and Tariffs

Trade barriers are government-induced restrictions on international trade, which can take the form of tariffs, non-tariff barriers, and outright bans. Conversely, a tariff is a tax imposed on goods as they are transported across international borders.

These factors can influence which goods are traded and how much those goods cost. Understanding these policies and how they affect trade is critical for strategic decision-making in international markets.

2.4. International Trade's Effect on the Global Economy

International trade has profound implications for the global economy, often leading to increased economic benefits for nations involved. With free trade, industries gain a competitive edge which can lead to increased production. Additionally, consumers benefit from a wider variety of goods and services that may not be available domestically.

Yet, there are also potential downsides. International trade can disproportionately harm some sectors within a country, particularly those involved in producing goods that are also mass-produced by competitors abroad.

2.5. Role of International Organizations in Global Trade

Certain organizations can facilitate, regulate, and supervise international trade across countries. Notably, the World Trade Organization (WTO), International Monetary Fund (IMF), and World Bank are integral to maintaining the infrastructure of international trade.

By providing guidelines for how trade should occur, resolving disputes between member nations, and offering financial support in certain conditions, these organizations help coordinate and manage international trade in an increasingly interconnected world economy.

2.6. Beyond Goods: The Rise of Global Service Trade

Traditionally associated with the exchange of physical goods, international trade now includes the rapidly growing service sector. These include banking, insurance, tourism, and software services, among others. The rise of service trade has led to new policies and agreements specifically catering to this sector, such as the General Agreement on Trade in Services (GATS).

2.7. Future Trends Shaping Global Trade

From e-commerce to environmental sustainability, several trends are expected to drive the future of global trade. Advancements in digital technology are simplifying cross-border transactions and opening new opportunities for global trade.

Moreover, an increased focus on sustainable and ethical practices within international trade is being seen. Going forward, understanding these trends will be critical for positioning oneself within international trade dynamics.

International trade is a vast and complex phenomenon, yet immensely rewarding for those who understand its ins and outs. Navigating this complex system might seem like a daunting task, but with comprehensive knowledge and strategic planning, thriving in this realm becomes a plausible goal. This richly detailed explanation of international trade's many facets, theories, and trends serves as a stepping stone towards unravelling the abundant opportunities that await in the dynamic world of global trading.

Chapter 3. Decoding Trade Agreements: A Wealth Builder's Guide

Trade agreements serve as the bedrock of international commerce, often dictating the terms under which businesses operate. Understanding these agreements is vital to unearthing and maximizing wealth-creation opportunities. This exploration will guide you through the important facets of an agreement and arm you with the knowledge to harness them.

3.1. Importance of Trade Agreements

Trade agreements have played an instrumental role in shaping global commerce. By simplifying and streamlining international transactions, they've diminished barriers, encouraging more robust trade relations. From an importer-exporter perspective, these agreements directly influence competitive landscapes by impacting costs, market size, and access to goods and services.

Understanding the terms, conditions, and opportunities embedded in these agreements can equip wealth-builders to interpret market changes, evaluate risks, and efficiently allocate resources. It also fosters the anticipation of regulatory shifts and can greatly aid in developing strategies for expansion and investment.

3.2. Anatomy of a Trade Agreement

Deciphering a trade agreement might appear daunting, given their comprehensive nature and legalistic language. Here are the primary elements you should focus on:

- Preamble: Sets forth the objectives, justifications, and spirit of the agreement.

- Definitions: Standardizes the interpretation of terms used within the agreement.

- Key Provisions: Areas of focus (e.g., tariffs, non-tariff barriers), each encompassing specific rules.

- Dispute Resolution Mechanisms: Procedures to mediate disagreements.

- Annexes, Attachments, and Footnotes: Provide further qualifications or explanations.

- Signature and Ratification: Formal agreement and acceptance by signatories.

3.3. Unveiling Tariff Concessions

The crucial part of any trade agreement wouldn't escape your notice—the provisions on tariff concessions. By reducing or eliminating tariffs on specified merchandise, countries aim to boost mutual trade and unlock economic growth. Understanding tariff schedules—how these reductions will be phased over time—is therefore pivotal for business planning.

Moreover, exporters should be knowledgeable about 'Rules of Origin'. These define eligibility for tariff concessions based on the product's origin. Incorrect assumptions about origin rules could lead to unexpected duties and compromise competitiveness.

3.4. Navigating Non-Tariff Barriers

While tariff concessions form the cornerstone of trade agreements, non-tariff barriers (NTBs) are equally consequential. These are measures other than tariffs that can influence trade. Licensing requirements, sanitary standards, quotas, and technical barriers to trade are some examples.

Comprehending NTBs often requires a meticulous assessment of the agreement text. The payoff comes in identifying new opportunities as countries open up sectors previously guarded by NTBs.

3.5. Leveraging Trade Facilitation Measures

Trade agreements are not just about tariffs and NTBs. They also contain measures designed to facilitate trade. Simplification, modernization, and harmonization of export and import processes represent some trade-facilitating strategies covered.

Knowledge about such provisions, such as pre-arrival processing, internet publication, and electronic payments, can facilitate smoother commerce and faster turnaround times, boosting your competitive edge.

3.6. Dispute Resolution Mechanisms

Inevitably, disagreements arise in the implementation of agreements. The 'Dispute Settlement Mechanism' section outlines processes for settling such issues. Given the potential of disputes to disrupt trade flows, understanding these procedures can aid in managing and mitigating trade risks.

3.7. Comprehending Trade in Services

Trade agreements have expanded to include provisions for trade in services, in addition to goods. This results in opportunities across sectors like telecommunications, finance, and e-commerce. Identifying these provisions can enable players in the service industry to leverage the benefits and establish a stronger foothold.

3.8. Understanding Intellectual Property Rights

In an increasingly knowledge-driven economy, protections for Intellectual Property (IP) can significantly impact trade. Understanding the IP clauses can protect your innovations abroad, align compliance activities, and avoid inadvertent infringement of others' IP rights.

3.9. Assessing Environmental and Labor Provisions

Increasingly, trade agreements include provisions on environmental and labor standards. These set the 'rules of the game' for sustainable trade. Being aware of these can help you align your business operations accordingly and avoid potential punitive measures.

Trade agreements indeed open doors to wealth-building opportunities, if you know where to look. By understanding their inner workings, tracking updates, and aligning your strategies accordingly, you can increase the odds of your global success. Keep learning, adapting, and growing in this vast world of international trade.

Chapter 4. Currency Trading and International Business: Minimizing Risk and Maximizing Return

Currency trading, alternatively known as forex (FX), is an integral cornerstone of international trade. When businesses venture into the global markets, understanding the nuances of currency exchange is pivotal to gauge both risks and returns. The goal here is to provide a comprehensive understanding of this realm, assisting you in both minimizing the anticipated risks and maximizing potential returns.

4.1. Understanding the Basics of Currency Trading

Currency trading, at its roots, involves the act of buying and selling currencies from around the globe with the intention of making a profit. The foreign exchange market (forex) is decentralized and operates 24/7 across different parts of the world. It's important to note, the forex market is influenced significantly by geopolitical events, macroeconomic data, and interest rate discrepancies between countries.

Businesses involved in international trade must ascertain the price they will receive in their home currency when exporting goods, or the cost in foreign currency when importing. This makes understanding the forex market crucial for these entities.

4.2. Identifying Currency Risk in International Business

Currency risk, or exchange rate risk, is an unavoidable part of international trade. It comes into play when a business deal is made in one currency, but the payment is due in another, exposing the business to the volatility of currency markets. Exchange rates fluctuate based on several factors - interest rates, inflation, political stability, economic performance, and speculation. If the home currency weakens against the foreign currency before the payment is made, the business incurs higher costs, impacting the bottom line.

4.3. Strategies to Minimize Currency Risk: Foreign Exchange Hedging

There are several options to protect your business from adverse currency shifts. The most common are hedging tools, like forward contracts and options:

1. Forward Contracts: A forward contract is an agreement to buy or sell a certain amount of foreign currency at a predetermined exchange rate, on a specific future date. This protects businesses from future exchange rate fluctuations.

2. Options: An options contract gives the right, but not the obligation, to buy or sell currency at a specific rate before a future date. This tool offers protection against unfavorable shifts but can benefit if the exchange rate becomes favorable.

4.4. Leveraging Currency Trading for Profit

Currency trading isn't only about managing risks but can also be used to accrue profits. Traders often leverage the differences in interest rates between two countries, a strategy known as the "carry trade." Here, one borrows in a currency with a low-interest rate and uses the funds to invest in a currency yielding a higher interest rate.

However, profits from forex trading aren't guaranteed and involve risks like interest rates' potential equalization over time and possible shifts in a currency's value against another. It's paramount to understand the dynamics of interest rates, monetary policy, and economic indicators before venturing into carry trade or similar forex strategies.

4.5. Spot and Future Markets in Currency Trading

Foreign exchange markets consist of the 'spot market,' where currencies are traded for immediate delivery, and the 'futures market,' where contracts are made to exchange currencies at a future date. Understanding the fundamentals of both markets is imperative. The spot market indicates the current value of currencies, crucial in pricing imported and exported goods. The futures market, by enabling you to lock the prices, alleviates the risk of currency fluctuations on future transactions.

As a wealth builder, knowledge of these markets will empower you to effectively make, manage and maximize your international investments.

Currency trading and international business form an interconnected sphere. This synergy, when understood and leveraged well, can open doors to minimized risks and maximized returns. International currency markets are complex, but with the right approaches and tools, you can navigate the waters of forex trading confidently and profitably. Balance risk management with strategic profit-making to make the most of your international business ventures. The world of global opportunity awaits, and armed with this knowledge, you are now better equipped to seize it.

Chapter 5. Investing in Overseas Markets: A Comprehensive Approach

Engaging in overseas investment comes with its fair share of advantages and risks. As a wealth-builder, your primary task is to understand these factors and how they influence potential returns. Mostly, it demands a well-thought-out strategy, and the aim of this chapter is to give you that strategy.

5.1. Understanding the International Investment Landscape

Before you choose where to invest, it's crucial to understand how different countries' economies function. This implies familiarising yourself with their economic policies, corporate laws, political stability, and market trends. Research is the most effective tool for this task.

A potential investor should assess the potential investment destination's political stability. Stable political conditions are conducive to strong, healthy economies and are likely to attract businesses and investors, ultimately promoting economic growth. Conversely, political instability can lead to the unstable economy, which can result in loss of investments.

Economic policies of your target country is another influencing factor. Policies that promote foreign investment are likely to result in profitable returns. On the other hand, policies that inhibit business operations could signal a high-risk market.

Corporate laws also need consideration as they dictate how businesses function in the foreign country. Clearly defined and enforced corporate laws provide a sense of security and are indicative of a healthy business environment.

Lastly, consider market trends. These refer to the widespread practices and behaviours in the marketplace and they offer indications on whether the market is suitable for your investment.

5.2. Evaluating Overseas Investment Opportunities

No two investment opportunities are the same, and the same goes for international opportunities. When it comes to evaluating these, you should look into details such as the market size, the level of competition, your potential for growth, and the type of client.

Market size is an initial consideration. A large market signals that there is a massive demand, therefore presenting potential for high sales. However, a smaller market should not discourage you as it also represents less competition.

The current level of competition can provide insights into market saturation. A market with fewer competitors may be more advantageous as it can allow for a larger market share. On the other hand, a large amount of competition may indicate a profitable market, but you need a unique selling proposition to thrive.

Evaluate your potential for growth. Look for markets which showcase trends, behaviour and demand for your chosen investment, as they indicate an excellent potential for growth.

Lastly, consider the type of client. Some businesses do better with a specific demographic. Understanding the customer persona can assist you in structuring marketing strategies and offerings.

5.3. Planning the Investment

Once you have an in-depth understanding of the landscape and have identified promising opportunities, the next step is planning your investment strategy. This involves careful consideration of the capital, projected returns, and a risk assessment.

Assess the capital requirements. Some investments may require substantial initial capital, while others may not. However, typically, sizeable investments tend to yield more significant returns.

Estimate the projected returns. This not only helps in understanding the potential profit but also serves to compare multiple investment opportunities. High return investments may appear attractive but they often carry larger risks.

Perform a comprehensive risk assessment. Understanding the possible threats to your venture allows you to anticipate and prepare for them, thereby, mitigating loss.

5.4. Implementing the Investment Strategy

After making these assessments, it's time to put your investment strategy into action. Whether you choose to invest in a startup, a running business, real estate or stocks, you need to understand the specifics of the venture.

Remember to always document your progress and revisit your strategy continuously in order to adapt and maximize the benefits.

5.5. Navigating Challenges

Investing in overseas markets is not without setbacks. Whether it be unstable political conditions, fluctuating exchange rates, or cultural barriers, being prepared will help you navigate these challenges. It is imperative to have a contingency plan for unforeseen circumstances.

The world is indeed filled with opportunities, but seizing them successfully requires not just capital, but knowledge. By understanding the overseas landscape, evaluating opportunities, outlining your plan, and being prepared for potential challenges, you can make international trade work for you. This sounds daunting, but with consistent efforts and diligence, it can lead to considerable growth of wealth and the expansion of your economic horizons.

Chapter 6. Breaking Down Language Barriers for Trade Success

Language comprises an integral part of human connection, facilitating communication and interaction. In the context of international trade, the importance of language becomes paramount. Its unique role in building cultural understanding and navigating business complexities cannot be overstated. It's a coin with two sides; hence, as much as language opens doors to potential business deals, it can also pose distinct challenges. With mastery, however, it can be transformed from a barrier into a bridge for trade success.

6.1. Understanding the Importance of Language in International Trade

Effective communication forms the backbone of successful business. In the wide, diverse scope of international trade, language barriers can profoundly influence the trade dynamics. A lack of language proficiency can often lead to miscommunications, misinterpretations, and misunderstandings that can erode trust and confidence, as well as mar business relationships.

Not only do these incidents lead to transactional challenges, but they also create potential risk in legal compliance. Laws and regulations differ across nations, and an understanding of trade law language is necessary to effectively navigate the international trade landscape.

One might argue that English, being the lingua franca of business, is sufficient. While English does command a dominant position in global affairs, the reality is that not everyone is proficient in English. By ignoring language diversity, businesses may inadvertently overlook attractive deals and valuable market insights.

6.2. Strategies to Overcome Language Barriers

Overcoming language barriers is not about acquiring fluency in multiple languages. Instead, it's about devising practical strategies and adopting technologies to improve communication flow. Here are a few universal strategies:

1. Learn Basic Business Terminologies: Understanding basic business terms and cultural nuances of your international partners can instill goodwill and establish a strong bond. Simple gestures like greeting in the local language can open the doors to better relationships.

2. Employ Translation Services: Professional translation services come in handy when venturing into a foreign market. While not all communication can or should be translated, legal and contractual documents must be accurately translated to understand the terms and conditions clearly.

3. Use Multilingual Staff: Having staff who are fluent in the language of your trade partners can be useful in handling negotiations, communicating, and doing business generally.

4. Leverage Technology: Digital technologies, such as AI-driven translation tools and language learning platforms, can be used to overcome language challenges. These can aid in real-time language translation, language learning, and even developing localized marketing strategies.

6.3. Cultural Sensitivity and Ethical Communication in Business

While the ability to communicate directly in a language is crucial, understanding cultural nuances and norms is equally essential. Effective communication is not merely about translating words verbatim. It also involves understanding intent, tone, body language, and context. Cultural sensitivity and ethical communication practices typically guide this.

Internationally, business norms and practices vary widely. What might be acceptable and standard in one culture could be considered rude or inappropriate in another. Therefore, understanding and respecting these cultural differences is crucial to succeed in international trade.

Several resources can guide your understanding of diverse cultural norms. Online courses, business guidebooks, and workshops can provide useful insights. Moreover, connecting with local business consultants or market specialists who understand the culture of the specific country you're dealing with can be exceptionally beneficial.

Applied ethically, these tools and strategies can make language an exciting opportunity rather than an insurmountable barrier. With cultural sensitivity, an understanding of the language, and the proper use of technology, it's possible to expand successfully into international markets. Your expertise in navigating language barriers will prove vital in your journey toward becoming a successful global entrepreneur.

6.4. Language Planning for Businesses

Language planning is a crucial aspect of international trade strategies. Corporate language policy should be an integral part of international business expansion plans. For instance, identifying the need for language training, investing in language learning resources, or hiring language consultants can be part of your strategy.

When planning for language use in international business, companies should consider:

1. Official Language: Is there an official language in the target market that differs from your home market? If so, how can you adapt?

2. Business Language: What language is commonly used for business transactions and meetings? Do you need translation or interpretation services?

3. Customer Language: What language do customers (or your target market) speak? Devise your marketing and communication strategy based on this information.

Remember, language planning is not a one-time process but requires consistent updating and revising with changing business and market conditions.

Despite the complexities and challenges, the ability to navigate language barriers effectively is a valuable skill in the realm of international trade, providing access to diversified markets and potential avenues of income and growth. As more and more businesses enter the global arena, the emphasis on overcoming language barriers has never been greater. With careful planning, cultural understanding, and strategic application, language can become a ladder to international success rather than a hurdle. Embark on this linguistic journey with patience, openness, and a learner's curiosity; the rewards are worth the effort.

Chapter 7. Trade Laws: Navigating Through Foreign Legal Waters

Entering a new market is an exciting prospect filled with opportunities, but also a matrix of legal issues. Navigating the foreign legal waters where trade laws are involved can be tricky. Our guide will help you find your way.

7.1. Understand The Legal Framework

Firstly, you need to get to grips with the overarching legal frameworks governing international trade. This includes International Trade Law itself, which covers the rules and customs for trade between countries. These norms are critical to understand, as they provide the foundation upon which countries base their specific laws for foreign trade.

Another integral piece of this puzzle is the international bodies that create, enforce, and administer the laws of trade. The World Trade Organization (WTO) is one of the most important. It's an intergovernmental organization that deals with the regulation of international trade between nations. Its principal objective is to ensure that trade flows as smoothly, predictably, and freely as possible.

7.2. Research National Laws

Next, begin researching the specific national laws of the country you wish to trade with. Each nation has its unique set of rules and regulations for business, including import and export restrictions, tax codes, and business law. Don't overlook environmental regulations and ethical standards either; these often come into play and can significantly impact your business.

Particularly, pay attention to laws around tariffs, quotas, embargos, and customs duties. Each country often has complex and diverse tariff systems, which can significantly affect the cost and feasibility of your business operations.

Keep in mind that compliance with tech regulations is also crucial in today's increasingly digital world. Regulations on data protection, cybersecurity, e-commerce, and electronic transactions vary widely across countries.

7.3. Familiarize Yourself With The Trade Agreements

Trade agreements are pivotal in shaping the landscape of international trade. Collaborations like the North American Free Trade Agreement (NAFTA), European Union (EU), Association of Southeast Asian Nations (ASEAN), among others, create powerful economic blocs that establish their trade rules.

Bilateral, trilateral, and multilateral trade agreements can also provide a solid base for your global expansion, offering preferential trade terms, providing access to new markets, and reducing trade barriers. The more you understand these agreements, the more effectively you can operate within their parameters.

7.4. Seek Legal Counsel

The process of navigating foreign legal waters should ideally involve seeking counsel from legal experts. This might be in the form of hiring an in-house counsel with expertise in international law, or contracting a law firm that specializes in international trade law matters.

Also, don't underestimate the value of local legal experts, who understand the intricacies of their nation's laws far better than any foreigners. They can provide valuable inputs on navigating the practical aspects of the law, predict legal challenges, and advise on all aspects related to cultural, socioeconomic, and bureaucratic factors unique to the nation.

7.5. Compliance And Ethics

Trade often goes beyond financial gains and losses; it can have broader economic, social, and environmental implications. From employing child labor or disregarding environmental standards to engaging in bribery or corruption, the ethical implications of business decisions are paramount.

Ensure that your business is complying with not only the letter of the law but also its spirit. Establish a comprehensive compliance program that goes beyond mere legalities and includes ethical aspects as well.

Adhering to the above guidance will surely help you sail through the foreign legal waters. It's an elaborate process, but with careful planning and execution, it can lead to valuable trade opportunities and significant business growth.

Chapter 8. Spotting Bubbles and Crashes: Safeguarding Investments Globally

Investing across borders offers sizable rewards, but it also comes with a unique set of risks. One of the most significant risks is market volatility due to economic bubbles and crashes. Learning to recognize these troublesome situations can be invaluable in safeguarding your investments.

8.1. The Anatomy of Economic Bubbles

An economic bubble occurs when the price of an asset or asset class significantly and continually exceeds its intrinsic value, typically as a result of speculative or frenzied demand. When the bubble bursts, prices plummet, investors panic, and a market crash may ensue.

Understanding the anatomy of these bubbles is critical for wealth builders. Essentially, bubbles tend to follow a relatively consistent five-stage process:

1. Period of Displacement: Innovations or changes in the economic environment displace established assets or sectors. New opportunities are created by this period of displacement.

2. Boom Phase: Prices rise slowly at first, but as more participants enter the market, prices start to climb at a faster rate.

3. Euphoria Phase: During this phase, asset prices spiral as speculators, drawn by the prospect of quick gains, rush into the market.

4. Profit-Taking Phase: The investors with more understanding of

the market realize that the asset is significantly overpriced and begin to sell off, taking their profits while they can.

5. Panic Phase: Prices plummet at a rapid rate, leading to a crash.

8.2. Recognizing Economic Bubbles

Recognizing an economic bubble is easier in theory than in practice, as it often involves a significant amount of market analysis and economic insight. Nonetheless, there are a few indicators that might suggest a bubble:

1. Rapid Increase in Prices: One of the most evident signs of a potential bubble is a rapid increase in asset prices, especially if the increase appears disproportionate to the intrinsic value of the asset.

2. Increased Media Coverage: Another common characteristic of a bubble is increased media coverage, with news outlets frequently reporting on the surge in prices.

3. Increased Market Participation: When everyone seems to be buying into a particular asset or asset class, this can be a sign of a market bubble.

Always approach markets with a healthy degree of skepticism, especially when prices seem "too good to be true."

8.3. The Anatomy of Market Crashes

Market crashes are sudden, steep drops in stock prices, often triggered by panic selling. They are generally the result of a burst economic bubble, an economic crisis, or a catastrophic event.

Crashes typically go through three stages:

1. The Precipitating Factor: Often an economic event or a significant

change in investor sentiment, this factor triggers the crash.

2. The Fall: As more people sell off their shares, the rapid withdrawal of buyers lead to a steep decline in prices.

3. The Aftermath: The market slowly stabilizes but with major changes. It can take years, or even decades, for the market to recover.

8.4. Spotting Market Crashes

While predicting the exact timing of market crashes is not an exact science, certain economic indicators can suggest an impending crash:

1. Overvaluation: If markets or specific stocks are significantly overvalued, this could be an indicator of a bubble and a potential crash.

2. High Leverage: When borrowers and investors take on more debt, it can indicate that they are overconfident in the stability of the market—this can signal a potential crash.

3. Economic Warning Signs: Negative GDP growth, high inflation rate, or high unemployment rates can be precursor signs of an impending crash.

8.5. Safeguarding Your Investments

Guarding against bubbles and crashes requires a well-rounded, long-term strategy:

1. Diversification: Diversifying your investments across different asset classes and geographical locations can help to mitigate the risks associated with individual markets.

2. Regular Monitoring: Regularly monitoring economic indicators and market health allows you to recognize trends and take corrective action early.

3. Knowledge and Education: Stay updated with global financial news and understand economic indicators. There's no substitute for education in navigating the complexities of the international investment landscape.

4. Financial Advisor: Consider seeking the advice of a qualified financial advisor. They can provide tailored advice based on your risk tolerance and investment goals.

Investing globally is no small endeavor, and the stakes are high. With careful preparation and sound strategies, it's possible to navigate the risky waters of international investment. Spotting bubbles and crashes is a crucial aspect of this preparation, allowing you to protect your portfolio from significant losses and capitalize on potential opportunities.

Chapter 9. Emerging Markets: The Untapped Goldmines

The economic dynamics of our world continue to pivot, with the tilt increasingly toward emergent economies. This presents a wealth of opportunity for advantageous engagement within this sphere, revealing unexplored territories abounding in potentials.

Emerging markets, colloquially termed the 'untapped goldmines', offer a multitude of opportunities for would-be wealth builders. These countries, generally characterized by rapid industrialization and economical developmental leaps, promise potential returns that outweigh those of mature economies. Yet, while the rewards seem promising, the path navigated to garner this success often looks less trodden and more obscure.

9.1. Deciphering the Dynamics of Emerging Markets

Understanding the essential features of these markets helps in comprehending just why they are considered unexplored goldmines. Firstly, these markets are characterized by strong, often double-digit growth rates in gross domestic product (GDP). Their economies are in acceleration, driven primarily by industrialization and modernization efforts. This growth creates investment opportunities across a wide range of sectors, from infrastructure and manufacturing to technology and services.

Secondly, because they are in the developmental stage, these markets present numerous areas of under-servicing and under-supply. Such an environment provides a fertile ground for entrepreneurs to start businesses and established companies to find new growth avenues. Furthermore, because the competition is usually less intense, the potential return on investment (ROI) can be immense.

Thirdly, the population dynamics in these countries often lend themselves favorably to economic growth. Many emerging economies have younger populations, which translate into a productive workforce rich in potential innovation, productivity, and consumption. This younger demographic is often a key driver for GDP growth.

However, it's imperative to remember that emerging markets are not without their risks. They often exhibit high volatility due to political instability, regulatory uncertainty, and infrastructural challenges, which can provide both opportunities and obstacles.

9.2. Identifying High-Potential Markets

Selecting an emerging market for investment necessitates meticulous analysis. The BRICS economies - Brazil, Russia, India, China, and South Africa - were the talk of the town in the last decade, demonstrating the shift of economic power away from the west.

Yet, a discerning investor needs to look beyond the familiar names, delving into the MINT economies - Mexico, Indonesia, Nigeria, and Turkey; or the VISTA economies - Vietnam, Indonesia, South Africa, Turkey, and Argentina. However, no single acronym can capture all high-potential markets, making due diligence essential in recognising the most lucrative opportunities.

Essential factors to consider during this analysis include:

- Economic indicators like GDP growth rate, inflation rate, unemployment rate, and industrial output.

- Political stability and government policies supporting foreign investment.

- Demographics, including the size of the population, median age, and income distribution.

- Market openness and ease of doing business.

- Infrastructure development and accessibility to vital resources.

9.3. Crafting an Effective Entry Strategy

Once a promising market has been identified, the next step is devising a robust entry strategy. This could involve direct investment, a joint venture with a local partner, franchising, licensing, or even acquisition of an existing local entity.

The choice of the entry strategy significantly depends on the market conditions, financial capability, required level of control, and risk tolerance. One needs to consider regulatory frameworks, cultural nuances, and market-specific intricacies in devising the strategy.

9.4. Navigating Risks and Challenges

Marginalizing the associated risks should be a major factor for any investor willing to tap into emerging markets. It's essential to conduct a rigorous risk assessment encompassing political, economic, financial, and market volatility risks.

For instance, political instability might jeopardize investments, whilst regulatory changes might affect profit potential. Currency fluctuations can impact the financial viability of an investment, while economic downturns can affect market demand. Adequate provisions should be made for such risks, including seeking professional advice and possibly obtaining insurance where necessary.

9.5. Harnessing Local Resources for Global Progress

Lastly, harnessing local knowledge and resources is vital in standing out among competitors. It's crucial to understand local cultural nuances, consumer behaviour, and market trends. Additionally, fostering strong relationships with local stakeholders – including government and regulatory bodies, business partners, and customers – can go a long way towards ensuring business success.

In conclusion, the emerging markets offer dazzling opportunities for wealth-building globally. However, they require more delicate handling due to the array of inherent risks. With careful navigation, a holistic understanding of the market dynamics, and strategic long-term visioning, these markets can indeed become untapped goldmines for generating wealth.

Chapter 10. Sustainable Trade: Linking Profits and the Planet

Sustainable trade recognizes the necessity of making a profit, while also understanding that it must occur in a way that does not harm the environment, public health, or social structures. Businesses are becoming increasingly aware that true, long-term success means integrating profits with principles - economic growth with environmental sustainability and social equality.

10.1. The Concept of Sustainable Trade

Sustainable trade is a modern approach to global commerce that seeks out a harmonious balance between economics and ethics. It aims to foster business activities that not only generate wealth, but also ensure the durability of our planet and uphold human rights. It operates on three core pillars: economic, environmental, and social sustainability.

Economic sustainability refers to creating stable, resilient, and robust markets. It encourages fair trade practices, competition, and appropriate regulation to protect consumers and businesses alike.

Environmental sustainability seeks to limit negative environmental impacts by promoting renewable energy use, efficient waste management, and responsible resource utilization. Avoiding the depletion of natural resources and aiming for a low-carbon economy are two additional key objectives.

Lastly, social sustainability promotes fair labor practices, equality, human rights, and social inclusion. It encompasses work safety, rights of workers, non-discrimination, and a fair distribution of wealth.

10.2. Sustainable Trade: A Business Case

Understanding sustainable trade in theory is the first step, but to fully grasp its significance, we must observe its application in business. A shift to sustainable practices offers immense benefits to businesses, often leading to increased profitability in the long term.

A sustainable model lowers operational costs through efficiencies in energy and resource use. With the right practices in place, businesses invariably reduce waste output and energy consumption, both translating to cost savings. Moreover, regulatory risks are mitigated as governments globally introduce stringent environmental laws.

Sustainable practices often result in improved brand reputation and customer loyalty. Consumers are increasingly seeking out businesses that show a commitment towards sustainability. This represents a significant opportunity to capture a growing market segment and increase market share.

Companies that integrate sustainable practices often reap benefits such as innovation and improved employee engagement. Necessity and novel challenges foster innovative solutions, often leading to novel products and services that differentiate the company from its competitors.

10.3. Interplay between Free Trade and Sustainable Trade

Free trade, a system based on lowering trade barriers like tariffs and quotas, is often seen as at odds with the principles of sustainable trade. The primary motive of free trade is economic growth, which can sometimes compromise environmental and social considerations.

However, it doesn't have to be this way. Free trade can lead to more efficient resource allocation globally and can contribute towards environmental and social sustainability. For instance, by allowing poorer nations to participate equally in global commerce, free trade can help alleviate poverty and promote social equality.

Similarly, free trade can stimulate green technology transfer between nations and foster the invention of environmentally friendly technologies. The key is to ensure that economic practices are built on a foundation of sustainability, creating a symbiotic relationship between free trade and sustainable trade.

10.4. The Role of Governments and International Institutions

The push for sustainable trade relies heavily on the proactive facilitation by governments and international institutions. They can shape international regulations and standards, set sustainability benchmarks, and enforce penalties for non-compliance. Incentives such as subsidies may also be set up to promote sustainable practices.

Institutions like the World Trade Organization (WTO) and United Nations (UN) play vital roles in connecting diverse nations to articulate and advocate for sustainable trade policies and regulations. They facilitate discussions, negotiations, and cooperation among nations to effect sustainable changes in global trade.

10.5. Examples of Sustainable Trade Practices

Finally, it is worth examining some real-life applications of sustainable trade practices. Businesses worldwide, from start-ups to established corporations, are changing their business models to integrate more sustainable practices.

Fair trade coffee farmers in Latin America, for instance, concentrate on organic farming practices that preserve the environment while receiving a fair price for their produce. Clothing companies are switching to organic cotton, reducing the water footprint, and ensuring better working conditions for their workers. Tech companies are finding ways to minimize electronic waste and enhance product life cycles.

Corporations like Unilever, Patagonia, and IKEA, to name a few, are leading the front in sustainable trade practices. Their efforts have not only resulted in a better ecosystem but have also translated to positive consumer response and financial success.

In conclusion, sustainable trade is not merely a trend, but a necessity in our rapidly changing world. It promises not only short-term gains but long-term resilience, prosperity, and preservation of our planet for future generations. Understanding and practicing sustainable trade holds immense potential for wealth creation and maintaining a business-friendly planet. This chapter aims to underline the significance of sustainable trade and hopes to inspire businesses and individuals to embrace this powerful concept.

Chapter 11. Future Markets: Understanding Tech Innovations in International Trade

To forecast the future, one must first understand the foundational changes that are happening today. Technology's omnipresence has redefined the way we conduct international trade, opening new avenues yet posing unprecedented challenges. This chapter delves into understanding how technology-driven innovations are shaping the future of global trade.

11.1. The Onward March of Technology

Technology is not only advancing; it's accelerating. The international trade sector is no exception, where various digital interventions have transformed the conventional business models. Consider e-commerce, for instance. Once a novelty, it is now a predominant mode of retail, connecting businesses and consumers worldwide. But where is this path taken us? Let's look at some key technological disruptions in international trade.

11.2. Electronic Trade Documents

The transition from paper-intensive processes to digital solutions has unlocked efficiencies unheard of before. Smart contracts, a product of Blockchain technology, have made a substantial impact in this respect. They are self-executing contracts, where the terms of the agreement are directly written into code. This brings in unprecedented transparency and security, significantly reducing the risk and time involved in document transfers.

11.3. Massive Data and Predictive Analytics

Never before has there been such an explosion of data generated every second across the globe, a situation coined as 'Big Data'. The availability of such massive data and the advent of analytics tools to process and interpret it have offered immense possibilities. They allow businesses to anticipate market trends, consumer behavior, and predict demand more accurately than ever. The predictive analytics is not a crystal ball, but it certainly gives an edge in decision-making and strategic planning.

11.4. The Role of IoT in International Trade

IoT, or the Internet of Things, represents a network of interconnected devices that communicate with one another through the internet. Be it tracking shipments in real-time, maintaining the right temperature for perishable goods during transit, or managing warehouse inventory, IoT is playing a pivotal role in simplying and optimizing trade processes.

11.5. Artificial Intelligence (AI) Revolution

Artificial Intelligence is another game-changer in international trade. AI has the potential to perform tasks faster and more efficiently than human counterparts, from customer service chatbots to automated driving systems in logistics. The implications of AI's continual development are vast, promising a future where manual and tedious tasks are automated, freeing humans to focus on complex and creative tasks.

11.6. Augmented and Virtual Reality

Remember, the technology that once seemed rooted in science fiction is becoming mainstream: Augmented Reality (AR) and Virtual Reality (VR). These revolutionary technologies provide immersive experiences, bringing value to businesses and consumers. Imagine a customer virtually trying products located miles away or visualizing how a piece of furniture fits their living room – that's the wonder AR and VR can bring in international trade.

11.7. Tech Innovations and Regulatory Environment

Granted, technology's benefits are immeasurable, but its pace poses significant challenges to regulators. How can laws and regulations keep up with rapidly evolving tech ecosystems? Governments, standard-setting bodies, and international institutions will need to create and adapt policies that promote innovation while protecting consumers and maintaining market competition.

11.8. Conclusion: Envisioning the Future

Merely understanding technology will not suffice in our rapidly changing world. Adapting to it, capitalizing on its power is the key to thriving in the future of international trade. Technology will continue to redefine the global trading landscape. Businesses that not only adapt but proactively plan for technology-fueled disruptions will undoubtedly be at the forefront of the global economy. To stay ahead, continuous learning is a must.

Remember, an open mind, an eagerness to explore new boundaries, and a relentless drive to turn obstacles into opportunities – these are the qualities that will allow you to tap into the exciting world of international trade. Embrace the technological revolution to become a successful wealth-builder in this era of global commerce.